THE JOURNALIST'S PRAYER BOOK

prayers by prominent
writers, editors
and newsmen

edited by
Alfred P. Klausler
and
John De Mott

AUGSBURG PUBLISHING HOUSE
Minneapolis, Minnesota

To all those journalists and others in the field of mass communications who through the years have been able to reconcile their faith — formal, organized, or otherwise — with the difficult and often challenging duties of a demanding profession

AUG 8 '73

THE JOURNALIST'S PRAYERBOOK

Copyright © 1972 Augsburg Publishing House

Library of Congress Catalog Card No. 72-78564

International Standard Book No. 0-8066-1231-2

Manufactured in the United States of America

CONTENTS

Preface 7

For Convictions of Steel: *John B. Cavanagh* 10

For Ability, Strength, and Courage: *John Quinn* .. 12

A Prayer for Wisdom: *Clifton Daniels* 15

Help Us, Father: *Louise Shadduck* 16

For the Will To See the Truth: *Roland E. Wolseley* 18

For Objectivity: *Robert Root* 19

To Write Responsibly: *John M. Drescher* 20

A Prayer for Strength: *Burton W. Marvin* 21

Prayer of a Managing Editor: *Edward M. Miller* ... 22

For Journalists: *Ralph David Abernathy* 23

Prayer of a Writer: *Harry Franklin Harrington* 24

On Facing a Blank Sheet of Paper:
  Darrell R. Shamblin 26

Help Me to Care: *George H. Muedeking* 27

Respect for Material and Honesty with Words:
  Henry Van Dyke 28

A TV Newsman's Prayer: *Walter Cronkite* 29

A Newscaster's Prayer: *Alfred P. Klausler*........ 30

For Insight and Constraint: *B. J. Stiles* 32

For Ethical Purpose: *Morris B. Margolis* 34

To Tell the Truth: *Maynard Shelly* 35

For an Editor's Struggle: *Charles Angell* 36

For Steadfastness: *Holt McPherson* 37

A Prayer for Perspective: *Mort Crim* 38

Prayer of the Religion Newswriters' Association:
    Lance Zavitz 40

Teach Us to Speak Truly: *G. Elson Ruff* 42

A Publisher's Prayer: *James A. Doyle* 43

Copy Editor's Prayer: *Ellen Soo Hoo*............ 44

For Words to Help Men Grow: *Ben Hartley*...... 45

A Prayer of Repentance: *Martin E. Marty*........ 46

A Journal Editor's Prayer: *Thomas F. Koerner* 48

A Foreign Correspondent's Confession:
    J. Laurence Day 49

For Fairness and Honesty: *Harold B. Walker* 50

For Editors: *Kenneth L. Wilson* 52

For Modesty: *Joseph L. Bernardin* 53

For Accuracy: *Benjamin McKelway* 54

For a Responsive Heart: *Balfour Brickner* 55

The Journalist's Creed: *Walter Williams* 56

To Be Faithful: *William B. Gray* 58

A Manuscript Reader's Prayer: *Walter MacPeek* .. 59

For Protection from Myself: *John De Mott*....... 60

For the Gift of Faith: *Albert J. Nevins* 62

At a Meeting of Journalists: *Grove Patterson* 63

For a Sense of Responsibility: *Oxie Reichler* 64

To Be a True Scribe: *Carroll E. Simcox* 65

The Stewardship of Language: *Ernest Mehl* 66

For a Good-Evil World: *LaRue W. Gilleland* 68

For the Divine Perspective: *W. C. Fields* 70

For Creativity: *Robert A. MacGill* 71

For the Power of Words: *Mrs. Harvey R. Herbst* .. 72

For Acceptable Work: *Carl E. Keightley* 73

Ten Commandments of Journalism:
   Charles H. Dennis 74

For the Writers of Words: *Vic Jameson* 76

A Magazine Editor's Prayer: *Walter G. MacPeek* .. 77

Mercy for an Editor: *Alan Geyer* 78

A Writer's Prayer: *Sherwood Wirt* 80

Prayer of a Prison Newspaper Editor: *Floyd King* .. 81

A Black Reporter Meditates:
   Millicent Brown Fauntleroy 82

A Columnist's Prayer: *Billy Graham* 84

A Travel Writer's Prayer: *Roger Swanson* 86

For Courage: *Lester Kinsolving* 87

A Prison Editor's Prayer: *Charles Clayton* 88

A Campus Newspaper Adviser's Prayer:
John H. Knowles 89

A Prayer for Newsmen: *James P. Clements* 90

For a New Beginning: *Louis Cassels* 92

A Suburban Editor's Prayer: *Paul D. Coffman* 94

A Newspaperman's Credo: *Max Lerner* 96

For Increased Sensitivity: *Helen T. Gott* 98

Combat Correspondent's Prayer: *Steve Bell* 99

For Guidance: *Eugene Patterson* 100

Go with Us in Our Work: *Dwight Marvin* 101

A Prayer to Recognize God: *Carl Lindstrom* 102

A Prayer for Peace: *Arthur C. Deck* 104

A Newspaper Editor's Prayer: *Felix McKnight* 105

A Broadcaster's Christmas Prayer:
Ralph W. Hardy 106

A Prayer of Gratitude: *W. A. Reed* 108

A Prayer for Endurance: *Richard K. Morton* 109

The Broadcast Newsman's Creed:
National Association of Broadcasters 110

A Prayer for Direction: *David B. Collins* 111

For a Sense of Vocation: *Based on Sarum Primer* . . 112

PREFACE

Somehow, over the years, those engaged in journalism — editors, reporters, photographers, radio and television newsmen, news magazine correspondents, and many others — have acquired a certain aura of irreverence. Perhaps it's because they have seen too much of the unsavory side of human nature and have also seen some of the skeletons in organized religion's closets. It becomes hard to hang on to religion of any kind. More often than not this irreverence is a prickly covering hiding a deep-seated commitment to a deity and to religious values.

For many years in the past, the professional press ignored religion as a subject of in-depth news coverage. The taboo against serious journalistic expeditions into the field of religion has been broken, however, in today's search for new values to guide man through our tortured age.

Looking back over our troubled past, the journalist feels a bit of remorse. Maybe more attention should have been paid to what was happening in the churches. Maybe instead of writing only about the clergyman gone wrong or the absconding church treasurer, the news media might have spent more time probing the convulsions and convolutions taking place in the church's theological processes.

And, if the profession of journalism had heeded religion's counsel to give more attention to the ethical dimensions of its service, perhaps the news media's current credibility would be greater. On the other hand, religion might—just might—be a more influential presence in today's world if it had shared journalism's concern for what is most relevant in the context of current events. All that is history. Now journalism and religion confront — together — a new age and its peculiar and perplexing problems.

For that challenge, we need a new vision of the good and the transcendent in human life. In his search for new values and their strength, the journalist can gain precious perspective from this book of prayers. Many of these prayers have been written by working journalists. Others have been prepared by clergymen whose insights and faith have inspired and comforted journalists.

Reading these prayers, the journalist can find encouragement, comfort, inspiration. Some of the prayers are sensitive in a personal manner. Others reflect a more formal dignity. Some look inward. Others are designed to communicate an understanding of journalism's special calling to a faithful stewardship of the truth of current events. Whatever the subject or mood, the prayers all reflect a living relationship with the eternal God.

8

Our thanks go to Association Press for permission to reprint from *The Student Prayerbook,* edited by John Oliver Nelson, the prayers on pages 109 and 112.

Individuals who provided generous assistance include Eric Sevareid — his **"fascination"** with the project served as a special inspiration — and these others: Robert U. Brown, David M. Butler, Dozier Cade, Turner Catledge, Jim Cesnik, George W. Cornell, Rob Downey, David J. Eisen, Joseph N. Freudenberger, Gene Giancarlo, Ray Hiebert, Russell Hurst, Charles F. Long, Harold Niven, Clarence O. Schlaver, Helen Thomasson.

Some of these prayers have previously appeared in a variety of professional journals and other publications. They are used, sometimes in adapted form, with the permission of the writers and editors. We trust there have been no oversights or errors. The identification of each author is his or her position at the time the prayer was written.

Finally, the editors thank Mrs. Sydell Reeves who faithfully typed and retyped the manuscript.

Alfred P. Klausler
John De Mott

FOR CONVICTIONS OF STEEL

Almighty God, the fountainhead of truth, give us convictions that are forged of steel, that cannot be bent or twisted or snapped by venal expediency, callous indifference, sanguine self-interest, or a cancerous betrayal of our trust as purveyors of truth.

The devil is no fool, and his recruiting program never stops. There are no coffee breaks in hell. His hours are the length of the day, and his years are the measure of eternity. In the beginning, he appropriately assumed a becoming image, a talking snake. He betrayed and won his first victim, a woman, and the lie became the badge and hallmark of every liar of both sexes from Adam and Eve to this atomic era.

We have succeeded in making our progenitors in the liars' sweepstakes look serenely angelic. There can be no such thing as virtue in any misrepresentation. The father of lies knows his disciples. He may give a knowing wink to the man who lifts a paper off the news stand without paying for it. He may give an encouraging smile to the man who plagiarizes a story or lifts a column. He may give a rattle of his tail to the man who pads his swindle sheet. Undoubtedly, he has a handshake for the man who lives a lie in sheer hypocrisy.

But he has a serpentine embrace for the newspaper-man who perverts the truth in his columns; who creates an ad that misleads or corrupts; who pollutes the clear stream of truth in news columns by injecting innuen-does, suggestive and inflammatory devices of deceit, and by leaving unsaid monuments to slander and character defilement.

May we not so much wonder whose side God is on, but with a renewed pledge to honesty and integrity, may we never wonder whose side we are on.

John B. Cavanagh, editor, *The Catholic Register*

FOR ABILITY, STRENGTH, AND COURAGE

Let us pray for the ability, the strength,
the courage, to resist
those who bully us for speaking sharply;
those who ridicule us for speaking with conviction;
those who berate us for speaking honestly.

Let us pray for the ability, the strength,
and the courage to overcome
those who want us to look but not see, and see but not
    look;
those who want us to listen but not hear, and hear
    but not listen to all;
those who want us to know but not understand, and
    understand but not know the facts.

Let us pray for the ability, the strength,
the courage to recognize
the propagandists who would use us;
the rascals who would abuse us.

Let us pray for the ability, the strength,
the courage to turn aside
those who want us to report all that titillates them;
those who want us to avoid all that annoys them;
those who want us to hide all that aggravates them.

Let us pray for the ability, the strength,
the courage to enlighten
those whose opinions get in the way of their facts;
those whose concerns get in the way of their
    competence;
those whose conclusions get in the way of their
    curiosity.

Let us pray for the ability, the strength,
the courage to rebuke
those who believe news is what is important to them;
those who believe trivia is what is unimportant to
    them;
those who believe importance is for them alone to
    decide.

Let us pray for the ability, the strength,
the courage to rebuff
those who argue that facts cannot speak for
    themselves;
those who argue that analysis must speak for them
    alone;
those who argue that opinion must be spoken at all
    times.

Let us pray for the ability, the strength,
the courage to fortify
editors who would abdicate to panels of amateurs;
editors who would hide behind committees of
    advisors;
editors who would forfeit their own rights and
    responsibilities along with the rights and
    responsibilities of the public.

Let us pray for the ability, the strength,
the courage to inspire
those who prefer power to responsibility;
those who prefer accolades to accomplishment;
those who prefer Grimm's Fairy Tales to the grim facts
    of full, fair, accurate news reporting.

John Quinn, executive editor, Gannett Newspapers

A PRAYER FOR WISDOM

I pray God to make
  me wise.
I'll take care
  of the rest.

Clifton Daniels, associate editor, *New York Times*

HELP US, FATHER

Help, Father, help!
Heavenly Father, help us to hold up before our readers
not our standard, or theirs, but the standard of Christ.
Help us to remember that it isn't what we write
that truly tells what we are.
Help us to remember that you can read between the
   lines
and know what is deep inside.

Help us so to write to instill confidence through truth.
Help us to give hope
where there is a lack of faith in our craft.
Help us to remember that our media are being
   challenged
to meet the problems of this day.
Remind us that our training may have been preparing
for just such a day as this.
Father, help us to leave the judgment to you.

Help us to be true to the moral code of Jesus,
which has been a beacon for 20 centuries.
Help us to teach it to those who follow us
and who are being handed experimental moral codes.
Help us so to live that those who follow will see
that the code of loving one another works.

Help us, Father, while we write of the thoughts and
words of others.
Father, help us.

Louise Shadduck, administrative assistant to
Rep. Orval Hanson of Idaho

FOR THE WILL TO SEE THE TRUTH

O God of grace, grant us the will to learn about the world and its people before we attempt to tell others about them.

Give us the patience to comprehend our complex society before we seek to explain it to our fellows.

Help us to develop standards in our daily work by which to measure our own actions as well as the actions of others.

Give us as reporters the ability to see matters as they are rather than as we want them to be.

Help us as editors to make our decisions for the good of all instead of for the monetary profit or special interest of the few.

Give us as journalists the courage to defend the rights and freedoms of all without abusing the freedoms possessed by our own profession.

Roland E. Wolseley, journalism professor, Syracuse University

FOR OBJECTIVITY

O Eternal Embodiment of Truth,
help each of us to see clearly the fine balance of justice
   and mercy
in disseminating news and opinion.

Help us to serve always the interests of truth and not
   of selfishness, whether our own or our friends'.

Help us to have courage to meet the needs of the
   minorities —
but of the silent majorities too —
remembering the rights of the little people in their
   myriads
as well as the elite who can punish or favor.

Help us to employ compassion in dealing with the
   news of those who suffer,
being fair with reputations according to a rule suited
to all reputations, including our own.

Help us ever to serve objectivity,
not as idol, but as symbol of the honest,
keeping ourselves detached, selfless, above narrow
   partisanship,
yet never confusing ourselves or our vision with thyself.

Robert Root, journalism professor, Syracuse University

TO WRITE RESPONSIBLY

Lord of all who labor long and late to communicate through the printed page, we come to you. Help us understand the meaning of "the word became flesh."

Forgive us when we sometimes assumed spectator seats and shouted from the bleachers or reported next day how the team goofed — without ever playing the game or getting next to those who feel the frustrations, fears, failures, and injuries of the struggle.

Teach us to write responsibly about the aches of our age: the pressing problems of the poor and the awful allurements of the affluent; the despair of the oppressed and the design of the oppressor; the sight of those who hunger and the sin of those who waste or do not share.

Give us a vision of what can and shall be, so that we may have at least some solutions to suggest for building a better church and world.

Help us to discern rather than bemoan the times, so that we may shed some light wherever darkness threatens.

Give us, O God, such confidence in you that fear and threats of man may never turn us from what we know we ought to say and do.

John M. Drescher, editor, *Gospel Herald*

A PRAYER FOR STRENGTH

Our Father, as journalism comes under attack from various directions for various reasons, help us to assess the rightness or wrongness of charges being made; to defend, resist and persist when we feel we are right; and to amend and reform when we are wrong. Above all, help us to respect and revere the vital role of journalism in our society by maintaining high standards of skill and attitude commensurate with this role. May we be ever mindful that our kind of work is most needed in times of crisis, and that in such times vying forces are most tempted to bring journalism under control for their own ends. Strengthen us that we may live up to the challenges both within our calling and outside of it.

Burton W. Marvin, journalism professor,
Syracuse University

PRAYER OF A MANAGING EDITOR

Oh Lord, may I find time to read the paper. May I be given will power to finish yesterday's unfinished business before I commence the new labors of this day. Give me strength to banish cranks who waste my time.

May I discern true worth in an applicant. May I extend full and patient attention to those of the staff who beseech me.

May fortitude and wisdom be sufficient to initiate and prosecute the fights for decencies that conscience requires. May the superior who selected me be content.

May I sleep well, though I stumble through the valleys of truth. May I be sensitive to the needs and wants of my community.

When watch of gold proclaims end of sweat, may there be joy in reflecting I envied no man his job, that what was done was somewhat near what might have been.

And may I accept with welcome grace the knowledge that men now young will discover better ways than I have known.

Edward M. Miller, former president, Associated Press Managing Editors Association

FOR JOURNALISTS

When I consider the profoundly critical responsibility of journalism to mankind, I remember my own calling to speak the truth at all times; and thus, I pray that the journalist shall speak the truth, for the truth shall set you free, as it will your audience and your readers.

Ralph David Abernathy, editor at large,
Christian Century

PRAYER OF A WRITER

Help me, O Lord, in a land of borrowed ideas to keep and develop what originality I already possess.

Make me more aggressive, more interested and alert in my daily contacts with people and with life, that I may find fresh material on which to write.

Increase, O Lord, my power to observe and feel and think, and to express my inmost thoughts with daring, incisiveness and pungency.

Forgive my indifferent spelling and my careless literary lapses, and prune my manuscript of faded phrases and dangling sentences.

Give me the courage to say resolutely, "I don't know," and then to go out unashamed to discover the right answer.

Help me to cultivate constantly at least one major interest, and to enjoy at least one recreation and hobby.

Give me an abiding pleasure in the arduous task of writing, keeping in mind always my obligation to win the interest of my reader.

Keep my mind well filled but never closed, and free me of conceit, buncombe, and pose, so that I may do my daily stint honestly and thoroughly, and without too much expectation of applause.

Let me not be too greatly discouraged by rejection slips, remembering that acceptance comes in the morning.

And when my typewriter is covered with dust, O Lord, add to my unfinished story a happy ending to all I have dreamed and thought and prayed.

Harry Franklin Harrington, director,
journalism school, Northwestern University

ON FACING A BLANK SHEET OF PAPER

Lord,
here I sit again at my typewriter
with a blank sheet of paper
staring at me.
It's hard to see the thousands "out there"
who seek some word
of encouragement, enlightenment, and inspiration.

Help me, a layman,
to be a minister today —
not a "preacher,"
but a "minister" of the written word.
Help me to share
thoughts profound in content,
but simple in language and style,
to encourage and assist others today
through the printed page.

May I remember
that my magazine isn't a place to parade my ego,
but a place where friends and strangers alike
may gather to visit, think, and share.
Guide my mind and my fingers today, Lord.
as I try to do my "thing"
to communicate "your way"
to all who live in your world.

Darrell R. Shamblin, editor, *The Interpreter*

HELP ME TO CARE

Lord, I suppose my biggest problem is, do you personally care whether I have any problems or not? Yet, even my work is based on a commitment that a man and his actions make a difference. Why else would I report a story if what men did wasn't worth caring about? Maybe it isn't so hard for you to care either, then.

Can the trouble be more serious? Am I pushing off on you what is truer of myself? Am I using my job description as an excuse, telling myself that what I'm reporting is no skin off my nose, saying that I can't be asked to care, since my only job is to tell the facts? Maybe that's why I suspect you'd want to do the same thing to me?

So help me to care more. Then I'll know you care about me too. After all, I do have your Son to show that what happens to us does make a difference to you. An eternal difference.

George H. Muedeking, editor, *The Lutheran Standard*

RESPECT FOR MATERIAL AND HONESTY WITH WORDS

Lord, let me never tag a moral to a tale, nor tell a story without a meaning. Make me respect my material so much that I dare not slight my work.

Help me to deal honestly with words and with people, for they are both alive. Show me that as in a river, so in a writing, clearness is the best quality, and a little that is pure is worth more than much that is mixed.

Give me an ideal that will stand the strain of weaving into human stuff on the loom of the real.

Keep me from caring more for books than for folks, for art than for life.

Steady me to do the full stint of work as well as I can; and when that is done, stop me. Pay what wages thou wilt, and help me to say, from a quiet heart, a grateful amen.

Henry Van Dyke, professor of English literature, Princeton University

A TV NEWSMAN'S PRAYER

Dear God:
help me remember
and my fellow man understand
that the truth knows neither friend nor enemy,
nor can those who pursue it.
Amen.

Walter Cronkite, newscaster,
Columbia Broadcasting System

A NEWSCASTER'S PRAYER

There are days, Lord, when that sweep second hand goes far too fast, and I'm reminded of my mortality, and I wish I could have written better, and articulated better, and told the truth, and maybe helped a few more people to see some of the glories and beauties in a world we have made sordid in so many places.

It's not only that second hand, but it's that red light on the camera staring me down. This may be you, Lord, reminding me to be short, sweet, to the point — and above all, honest. Too often have I smiled or dropped my voice in a fake, confidential tone when I should have frowned, maybe even sneered, and screamed over the fakeries of politicians and generals.

I need strength, Lord, because there are times when the clash of events comes too fast over the machines, and I can't always sort out the important and true from the trivial and false. Forgive me for all my failures and give me the strength to exercise good judgment at all times.

Remind me again and again that your people listen and watch what I'm doing. They are good and bad people, young and old people, bright and stupid people, rich and poor people. But they're all your people; let me never needlessly hurt them.

I do wish, Lord, you could make that second hand move a bit slower because I just can't say everything that needs to be said.

Alfred P. Klausler, religion commentator, Westinghouse Broadcasting Company

FOR INSIGHT AND CONSTRAINT

O God, who art the word of life, accept our words as responses to thy truth. May our writing be seen as messages of thy hope for all mankind.

We thank thee for quotable leaders, and votable readers — and pray that we may restrain ourselves from exploiting both for our own private causes.

Grant us the insight to expose the charlatans, and the courage to depose the demagogues — and enlighten us that we become neither.

Constrain our cynicism, and give us cause to expand our optimism. Grant us the wisdom to mitigate our dogmatism, and a vision to transcend our parochialism.

Purge our platitudes by the fire of history, and redeem our clichés by revealing free men who speak the truth freshly and clearly.

Where we have shrouded joy and idealism by our own crepe-hanging, forgive us. Where we have misled by half-truths and managed views, restore us. And where we have tired of the fight and turned to less costly issues, give us strength.

Redeem the arrogance of affluence through the simplicity of human kindness and the restoration of social justice. Penetrate the mirage of our greatness through the cry of the exploited and the anger of the dispossessed.

This we ask of thee, the source and model of all creation.

B. J. Stiles, editor, *motive*

FOR ETHICAL PURPOSE

When honesty moves our pen, O Lord,
you move it.
When integrity fashions our thoughts, O God,
you fashion them.
When compassion shapes our syntax, O Father,
you shape it.

May we ever be your associates
in the vast editorial chamber
which is your universe;
may our galleys emerge untainted by moral error;
may our cases —
both lower and upper —
pass the test of your divine scrutiny;
and may the proofs of our ethical purpose
reside in the enlightenment we may bring
to the minds and hearts
of our fellow men.

Morris B. Margolis, rabbi, Kansas City, Mo.

TO TELL THE TRUTH   1766453

Today, the words were not too pleasant, Lord.
"You got us in a mess with what you wrote,"
they said. "Let's see you get out of it."
Oh, yes; we made them angry once before,
but then they came to us in ones and twos.
The injured folks are organizing now.
With signed petitions, they will shortly come.
So this is what it's like when one is scared.

A writing talent I may really have,
but do I have the guts to face the noise,
to tell the truth and clearly call the shots?
Perhaps my words could have a softer shade,
but dare I cut and run when under fire?
My friends have gone to jail for praying in
the streets. And others give their lives to
working with your broken poor. Those words on
paper cost a lot. When all around me lose
their nerve, help me to write and bear the cross.

Reward enough for me will be to know
that truth has lived another day.

Maynard Shelly, editor, *The Mennonite*

FOR AN EDITOR'S STRUGGLE

Dear Lord, keep me in your truth. Sometimes I'm looking for a headline and the substance slips away from me. Help me to tell it like it is. No more, no less.

Keep me in your love. I get mad at all those "Letters to the Editor" that call me every name in the book. Let me never fall out of love with those who disagree with me.

Help me with your struggle. Sometimes I think that every black face in my magazine is a threat to my circulation; every sentiment for international cooperation a nail in my coffin; every disagreement with my bishop a step towards retirement. Let me never fail to say what I honestly think is the truth after mature reflection.

And finally, dear Lord, let me share your sense of humor. Surely you must have one. And there are many days when I feel that the business of religious journalism is just as crazy as the business of creation and redemption.

Charles Angell, editor, *The Lamp*

FOR STEADFASTNESS

O God, who rulest the worlds from everlasting to everlasting, speak to our hearts when courage fails. Men faint from fear, and the love of many grows cold, and there is distress of the nations upon the earth. Keep us resolute and steadfast in the things that cannot be shaken, abounding in hope and knowing that our labor is not in vain indeed.

Restore our faith in the omnipotence of good and in the love that never fails. And make us to lift up our eyes and behold the things that are seen and temporal, and the things which are unseen and eternal, through Christ, our Lord.

Holt McPherson, editor, *High Point* (N.C.) *Enterprise*

A PRAYER FOR PERSPECTIVE

Help us, God, never to become so bewildered by the happenings of the moment that we lose the perspective of history. As newsmen, the moment is our business. The event. The occurrence. Ours is a right-now profession. There are far too many deadlines and far too little time for reflection and contemplation. Help us to see the experiences we report against the backdrop of eternity. Without such perspective, we tend to become cynical and despairing.

May we bring the hard questions of our day before the public consciousness without, ourselves, becoming hardened or bitter. Keep us aware that truth lies beyond the bulletins and the headlines—that no matter how important our immediate assignment may seem, the biggest story is man himself, his dreams and his destiny.

Sharpen our perception, so that we may see what is. Sharpen our abilities, so that we may faithfully reflect what we see. Repair the biases and remove the prejudices which would prevent us from clear and honest reporting.

But never let us be content with merely reflecting. Grant us wisdom to generate some light of our own. We would deepen our commitment to relevancy and understanding; for if our first responsibility is to tell it like it is, our second is to explain what it means.

Give us the will to seek and the courage to report the truth about the facts—to explain, to highlight, to underscore, and to clarify.

May our minds be always sensitive to injustice as well as to error. To the extent that injustice is born of error, may our talents be always employed in eliminating both.

Mort Crim, news commentator, WHAS, Louisville, Ky.

PRAYER OF THE RELIGION NEWSWRITERS' ASSOCIATION

Eternal Father:
We are they who worship thee with typewriters instead of altars and the odor of ink for the sweet savour of incense.

We come now before thee, seeking approval for that which we have done, asking thy guidance in that which we are about to do, and praying for thine inspiration in those things we hope to accomplish.

O thou who didst reveal thyself in him who said, "I am the truth," we cannot separate ourselves from our work, our writing from our lives. That which we ask in relation to our writing, we ask also in relation to our living.

Give us wisdom to know the truth, courage to write the truth, and strength to stand fast against all that would lure us from the way of truth.

Grant that our writing may reflect thy truth, as even the smallest fragment of glass may catch the rays of the sun and send them darting into the dark and gloomy places.

40

Forbid that we should ever sacrifice the truth to serve the well-turned phrase, or that we should obscure its radiance with careless words.

Yet give us, we beseech thee, the sympathy that tempers truth to gentleness and makes of righteousness a warm and friendly thing.

When thou dost scan what we have written—and perchance have left unfinished—wilt thou, we humbly pray, end the story with thine own skilled hand, and in thy mercy write a "30" to it!

Thou wilt find many a clumsy phrase and ill-chosen word. There will be here and there a dash, because we could not find the words to say what was in our hearts. The story would be the better for complete rewriting.

But when the self-appointed copy readers frown, and sigh, and point to awkward word and crudity of phrase, wilt thou, in thine infinite wisdom, grant us this one more boon? Wilt thou say:

"This, with all its imperfections, is the true story of a sincerely loving heart. Let this story run!"

Lance Zavitz, religion news editor,
Buffalo Evening News

TEACH US TO SPEAK TRULY

Our Father, who hast spoken the eternal Word by which we are led into truth, teach us to speak truly in our vocation as journalists. Give us clear sight into things as they are and courage and wisdom in stating facts honestly and cogently. Help us to interpret the confusing events of our time. Safeguard us against cynicism. Freshen us in our work with the constant renewal of thy presence. Let us close each day in quiet trust and confidence, through Jesus Christ thy Son our Lord.

G. Elson Ruff, editor, *The Lutheran*

A PUBLISHER'S PRAYER

Lord, let us help men to know fully, so they may judge rightly, and knowing the right way, act with vigor and with justice.

Let the materials we publish be ennobling for man's spirit, mind, and body.

Help us to employ with social fairness and awareness those professionals, in all staff positions, we need to do our most effective work.

Help us to learn and employ today's techniques and tools, so we may compete successfully.

Let us research our material with care, write with honesty and concern for all mankind, edit with precision and talent, publish with wisdom and acumen, distribute successfully and as widely as we're able, and thereby bring truth and love to our readers, while serving the whole community of man, and you, Lord.

James A. Doyle, executive director,
Catholic Press Association

COPY EDITOR'S PRAYER

Lord, please give us

wisdom to exercise sound judgment in editing copy and writing headlines,

humility to admit honest mistakes,

a thick skin to withstand criticism from reporters who think that we've butchered their copy,

cleverness to inject a bit of wit into dull, lifeless copy and headlines but restraint from sensationalizing the news,

the energy and desire to keep up with the day's news from around the world,

and finally, since technology has not invented a rubber type which is pliable, help us to withstand the aggravation which comes when heads just don't fit.

Ellen Soo Hoo, staff writer, Illinois Medical Program

FOR WORDS TO HELP MEN GROW

In this world full of words, O God, make us aware of the meaninglessness of words which are not imbued with the spirit of your Word. Convict us of our sin of intellectual arrogance and the resulting failture to communicate your Good News to the world. Make us humble, for our sloth and professional incompetence have truly profaned your holy name. Forgive us, Lord, for our lack of courage to speak and write the truth, and perhaps most of all we need your forgiveness for our failures to do what we say. But if it is your will, O God, take these miserably inadequate expressions of our faith and use them in whatever way you will that men may grow in the knowledge of your grace, mercy, and everlasting love.

Ben Hartley, editor, *Presbyterian Survey*

A PRAYER OF REPENTANCE

Let me see, now ...

I'd better begin with repentance. It's an old habit, and like a logical place to start. As everybody else, I like to think of myself as being faultless (or at least as being capable of sneaking past scrutiny) but that never works for very long. Turn around. Re-turn. Dear God, there is room for both, if I am to be open to change and, while humanity may never notice it, to improvement.

Humanity? Let me cut it down to size: some people, at least, have seen and will see what I have done and will do. I don't mean the minor errors; typoes, syntactical goofs, inelegancies in general. (Though on paper, as like in spiritual life, the good can be nibbled and nickled-and-dimed to death.) I *do* mean the profound errors. I must call them misdeeds sins. Sins of misstatement and overstatement, of known distortions and unexamined attitudes which can produce unrecognized distortions. Forgive me for all the times I have overlooked the need of the other, have deprived others of their potential—and thus, of their humannes.

46

Let me be open to the stirrings of grace, so that I may be free for service through this medium and so that its message may help bring Christ's freedom to some segment of the world.

May the Lord have mercy on the circulation department. And God bless my copy editors.

Martin E. Marty, associate editor, *Christian Century*

A JOURNAL EDITOR'S PRAYER

My writers, O Lord, are contributors all—be they administrators, professors, or supervisors. Yes, they are erudite, intelligent, experienced without question.

But yet, I beseech thee, help them to express their ideas; let them not be discouraged by the beauty of simple, concise, and clear language.

Help them to see statistics, chi-squares, and surveys not as ends in themselves, but as necessary tools. Help them to understand that results, not methods, comprise the ingredients of meaningful articles. Help them simply to write for the reader, to know the challenge of interesting the least interested.

This, O Lord, is the request of the editor who reads first for the reader's needs.

Thomas F. Koerner, editor, *Bulletin* of the
National Association of Secondary School Principals

A FOREIGN CORRESPONDENT'S CONFESSION

The Defense Ministry lines were busy. It was raining outside so I wrote:
"Informed sources report . . ."

The Ambassador's wife snubbed mine, so I wrote:
"Worsening diplomatic relations are evident across . . ."

Amazon, Inc. put me on a private plane and flew me to their plant and then to a resort. And I wrote:
"One of the most exciting commercial ventures in many years has . . ."

The complexities of the political situation baffled me, but I wrote:
"The reason for the political chaos in this country can be summed up very simply—greed."

The police confiscated one issue of the world's greatest newspapers, *El Diario Grande,* and I wrote:
"The iron fist of censorship struck another blow against the freedom of the press today. . . ."

Police raided *El Diario Chico,* a leftist rag, and closed it down and threw its editors in prison, I wrote:
Nothing.

God forgive me.

J. Laurence Day, journalism professor,
University of Kansas

FOR FAIRNESS AND HONESTY

Eternal God our Father, we are grateful for gifts of mind that enable us to think and write with clarity, and for the privilege of reporting and interpreting the news of the day. Grant us grace to compose with integrity of spirit and fidelity to the truth. Enable us to write with fairness and honesty, and grant us courage to risk the unpopular on the altar of our sense of responsibility. Sustain us, O God, with thy strength and keep us steadfast in purpose.

Keep us aware of thy presence wherever we toil together in the service of our time, wherever truth is honored and justice sought, wherever typewriters tap and presses whirl to disseminate knowledge free men ought to know. Thou art not far off beyond the mists of the Milky Way, O God, but nearer than breathing where two or three or many link their minds and lives to serve the common good.

Guard us, our Father, lest our prejudices corrupt our insight and pervert our capacity to see things as they are; protect us when our interests threaten our integrity; preserve us from the temptation to use our skill with words to make the worse appear the better part; and make us willing to spend ourselves beyond the call of duty to find the facts behind the facades that hide the truth.

Enable us in all we write to honor the dignity of human kind, to protect the weak and the helpless, to defend the unjustly accused, to expose the powerful who prey upon the poor and the unlearned, to uncover the corrupt that hides behind the pretenses or respectability.

We would be worthy of our high calling, O God, loyal to the best we know in Jesus Christ our Lord.

Harold B. Walker, religion columnist, *Chicago Tribune*

FOR EDITORS

O God, how nimbly we have learned to sidestep the pressures that would sweep us from the reviewing stand into the line of march. We have enjoyed our official spectator status. We have been often tempted to thank you that we are not as other men are; that we, by turning down our windshield visors, can park where others cannot park; or by showing press cards, go where they cannot go; or by being ruthlessly single-minded, can invade minds with our ideas.

God, be merciful to us who have never revealed ourselves, never shared ourselves, or who have considered the account of the story more important than the story itself. Let our powers grow out of our ability to identify with all men, and not out of our skill at separating ourselves from them. Let our readers feel because we have first felt, see deeply because we have seen deeply, ache because we have ached, hear because we have heard.

As the turmoil of life flows through our minds, let it leave its mark upon us that we may leave our mark upon it. In the name of him who dares to ask *us*, "Who do *you* say that I am?"

Kenneth L. Wilson, editor, *Christian Herald*

FOR MODESTY

Grant unto us, O Lord, the gift of modesty. When we speak, teach us to give our opinion quietly and sincerely. When we do well in work or play, give us a sense of proportion, that we be neither unduly elated nor foolishly self-deprecatory. Help us in success to realize what we owe to thee and to the efforts of others; in failure, to avoid dejection; and in all ways to be simple and natural, quiet in manner, and lowly in thought; through Christ.

Joseph L. Bernardin, general secretary,
National Conference of Catholic Bishops

FOR ACCURACY

O Lord, please deliver us from bad reporting and bad editing. Please make everybody connected with our newspapers understand how important readers are — far more important than the editors. Give us reporters, O Lord, who spurn rumors and respect only fact. And surround them with editors, O Lord, who are as good as the reporters.

Make the people who run newspapers, O Lord, understand that the good people of this country really depend upon them for accurate news. Tell them, Lord, that every time the papers make fools of themselves by mistakes, juvenile excitement and undue preoccupation with the trivial they lose something of their most precious asset — the confidence of their readers. Let them know that it is upon this confidence that freedom of the press depends. It does not depend upon what politicians say or do.

Purify us, O Lord, of the cynics, the gossip mongers, the dangerously irresponsible and unthinking — all of those who lack respect for an honorable calling and bring shame upon its good name. Remind us that our job is to find the truth, and after finding it, to print it.

Benjamin McKelway, editor, *Washington Star*

FOR A RESPONSIVE HEART

Master of All Eternity, we stand before Thee, now as always, in awe and in humble gratitude. For thou hast laid numberless gifts and blessings in our cradle as birthrights: concern by which to see care, thought by which to gain knowledge, intelligence by which to gain wisdom.

Help, O God, those who influence the lives and thinking of others, that we might always be men and women passionately devoted to objective truth. Above all other interests — sectional, national, and personal — may we see ourselves as forces in society whose influence must always be towards the goals which affirm and conserve life rather than to that which might deny or destroy it.

As thou has blessed us with mind, bless us, O God, always with the greatest gift, the gift of a sensitive and a responsive heart.

Balfour Brickner, rabbi, Washington, D. C.

THE JOURNALIST'S CREED

I believe in the profession of journalism.

I believe that the public journal is a public trust; that all connected with it are, to the full measure of their responsibility, trustees for the public; that acceptance of a lesser service than the public service is betrayal of this trust.

I believe that clear thinking and clear statement, accuracy, and fairness are fundamental to good journalism.

I believe that a journalist should write only what he holds in his heart to be true.

I believe that suppression of the news, for any consideration other than the welfare of society, is indefensible.

I believe that no one should write as a journalist what he would not say as a gentleman; that bribery by one's own pocketbook is as much to be avoided as bribery by the pocketbook of another; that individual responsibility may not be escaped by pleading another's instructions or another's dividends.

I believe that advertising, news and editorial columns should alike serve the best interests of readers; that a single standard of helpful truth and cleanness should prevail for all; that the supreme test of good journalism is the measure of its public service.

I believe that the journalism which succeeds best — and best deserves success — fears God and honors men. It is stoutly independent, unmoved by pride of opinion or creed of power, constructive, tolerant but never careless, self-controlled, patient, always respectful of its readers but always unafraid. It is quickly indignant at injustice. It is unswayed by the appeal of privilege or the clamor of the mob; it seeks to give every man a chance, and, as far as law and honest wage and recognition of human brotherhood can make it so, an equal chance. It is profoundly patriotic while sincerely promoting international good will and cementing world comradeship. It is a journalism of humanity of and for today's world.

Walter Williams, dean, journalism school,
Missouri University

TO BE FAITHFUL

Almighty God, we give you thanks for the power of
  speech,
for the power to put our words into print,
for the power to send our words around the world,
for our own abilities to write and to edit what others
  have written.
We ask you to continue us in our task,
to help us to be courageous and truthful,
not to fear conflict,
and always to be faithful to you
in presenting news and opinions.
We ask in the name of your Word.

William B. Gray, editor, *Virginia Churchman*

A MANUSCRIPT READER'S PRAYER

Today I ask, O Father, that I may be an encourager.
that I may find some glimmer of promise
which I may encourage to grow;
Grant me the strength to be generous
in my words of commendation;
Give me the perceptiveness and the insight
to respond to thoughts that may touch the heart,
as well as the mind.

Grant that today I may find much of worth:
writers who have something to say and who say it
    simply,
whose writing is clear and uncluttered,
whose tone is warm
and whose writings are rich
in illustration and anecdote,
whose writings leave no ribbons of rhetoric
to flutter in the eyes of readers,
whose manuscripts have a beginning and an end
and stop when the end is reached.

This is much to ask, Great Father,
but the need is great
and thy heart is unlimited.

Walter MacPeek, author, New Brunswick, N.J.

FOR PROTECTION FROM MYSELF

Eternal Spirit of Truth,
make me a skeptic.
Teach me to doubt the easy answers — the lazy ways
of explaining any news event.

Help me to appreciate the full range of human gulli-
bility and ignorance — most of all, my own.

Embolden me to ask the tough questions, and to seek
the hard answers.

Set me upon the straight and narrow way which leads
to specificity, and greater accuracy.

Reveal to me the concrete facts, and deliver me from
the delusions of ill-founded faith and the bonds of
ideology.

Grant me patience for the slow winnowing of tedious
details, and the inspiration for the long hours of hard,
dirty work which lie between any news event and its
complete reporting.

Sustain me through the painstaking process of testing my assumptions—ruthlessly—against an event's reality.

Most of all, I pray, give me the insight to challenge my most cherished beliefs and preconceptions.

Protect me from myself, bestowing upon me an ability to cultivate those doubts toward my own philosophy which the newsman calls his journalistic objectivity.

It is not given to men, we know, the power to be 100 per cent objective. But the measure of any newsman, we also know, must always be the degree to which he approaches that ideal.

Teach me humility, compassion, and consideration for those forced by news events to throw themselves upon my typewriter's mercy.

Enable me, somehow, to treat those involved in the news as I would want them to treat me: to make religion's Golden Rule the standard for journalistic ethics, as it is for personal morality.

And forgive me, each day, each error of either omission or commission in reporting that day's news.

John De Mott, journalism professor,
Northern Illinois University

FOR THE GIFT OF FAITH

Almighty God, who gives to each man his talents, not only for one's own welfare but for the general betterment of all mankind, remind us once again that our skill with words can serve no greater cause than truth, justice, and individual freedom.

Keep us ever aware that principle cannot yield to expediency; that the might of words is in building and not in destroying; that the powers with which you have endowed us must never be used against your will.

Grant us appreciation of the fact that in working on men's minds, we are working on eternity. Bestow on us the gift of faith in our work, faith in ourselves, and faith in our fellow men.

Enable us to replace doubt with knowledge; enmity with love; sadness with happiness; falsehood with truth, so that when the time comes for our personal "30," we shall through the talents which you have given us leave this world a little bit better than when we came into it.

Albert J. Nevins, editor, *Our Sunday Visitor*

AT A MEETING OF JOURNALISTS

Almighty God, we pause for a moment at the beginning of this meeting to give expression to our gratitude for blessings, some of them peculiar to America, for which we have been insufficiently appreciative.

We are grateful for the privilege of free expression. But may we be mindful of the moral responsibility which marches with that privilege.

In the deliberations of these hours to come, may we be released from bickering, from pettiness, from ill-advised attention to trivialities, from the temptations of injustice, and from every aspect of unkindness in our decisions.

As we here seek light, and in our living day by day, may we become more acutely aware that our finest ideas derive from a power greater than ourselves. May we seek to have communion with that power. In a renewed faith may we seek to translate ideals into reality.

Finally, we pray for humility, remembering the words of the prophet:
"For what doth the Lord require of thee but to do justly, to love kindness, and to walk humbly before thy God."

Grove Patterson, editor, *Toledo Blade*

FOR A SENSE OF RESPONSIBILITY

Dear Father of us all, source of all our freedoms, guide us by your holy light and your truth so that we may fulfill the biblical injunction to "proclaim liberty throughout the land unto all the inhabitants thereof." Help each of us to search for, to find, to ennoble, and to share the truth in every way on every day; to winnow fact from fancy; to use well our powers of reason and logic, good sense, and fair play.

Fire our hearts with the highest sense of personal and public responsibility, with imagination and kindness, with courage and determination, with mental discipline and moral fortitude, with charity, humility, and faith — faith in the ultimate goodness and justice of your Word.

Inspire us always to keep the press a servant of the public, seeking to generate the dynamic power of an informed free people, leading them to constructive action.

Teach us to find true freedom by striving for the freedom of others, as men and women of good will have done throughout the ages. In freedom and in peace, dear Lord, may we help break bonds of ignorance that shackle and debase the spirit of man.

Oxie Reichler, editor, *Yonkers* (N.Y.) *Herald-Statesman*

TO BE A TRUE SCRIBE

Lord Christ, you are the Word of the Father from everlasting to everlasting, and you have taught us that for every idle word we speak or write we must answer in the day of judgment.

So guide me in your way, show me your truth, fill me with your love, and so rule my heart and direct my mind as I write, that my words may glorify you, the Word of life, by enlightening all who read them.

I want to be a true scribe of your kingdom. Enable me by your grace to be one.

Carroll E. Simcox, editor, *The Living Church*

THE STEWARDSHIP OF LANGUAGE

O Lord of creation, thou hast made thyself known to us through thy word; for words can be creative, and those who create thy kingdom with words have an affinity with thee.

To these is given the joy which comes in the creation with words of good rather than evil, of love rather than hate, of hope rather than despair, of happiness rather than sorrow.

As thy Word became flesh in Christ, so our words can become life rather than death. Words can challenge rather than discourage. They can ring with the clarity of a bell or sound hollow and meaningless.

We have been granted the use of words so that we, too, can create, and we know, our great God, that when one creates he is in tune with thy universe.

Words can sound the challenge which can lead all mankind to thee. They can reveal that which is hidden; they can point to the road which our Master walked and to the truths which he alone understood.

We are inheritors not only of his peace, but of his Word, trustees of that Word, for words have brought understanding to the confused, knowledge to the uninformed, assurance to those who waver.

Yet words also have created doubts and envy and malice and distrust. So may we use each word as we would a precious gem — thoughtfully, carefully, considerably, honestly, remembering that Jesus used words and he gave them life and he lighted them with such a compassion that they will live forever.

We know that every word we use is edited finally by a God who has given us his own style book and who is far more concerned over the words which come from our hearts than those which issue from our lips.

In the beginning was the Word. We, who work with words, pray in his name.

Ernest Mehl, former sports editor, *Kansas City Star*

FOR A GOOD-EVIL WORLD

Ultimate God,
few will conclude from today's news
that the world is all good;
but deliver us
from the debilitating thought
that it is essentially evil.

If it is your will,
comfort us who are paid to observe and write
with the understanding
that we see the world one way or another
largely by the frame of reference
in which you place us.

Comfort us with the understanding
that even with your omnipotence,
creation and perfection of a universe
in time and space may, by necessity,
take a moment in time.

From our prospect
on a tiny particle of the vast cosmos,
that moment — in which imperfection, disease,
pain, controversy, war occupy
our working lives — may appear
to be very long.
But from your perspective, God,
that moment may be
infinitesimally brief.

Help us to comprehend
that seeing the world as fundamentally evil
is seeing it from the position of suffering man;
that seeing it as fundamentally good
is positing the point of view of God.

If both views are real, the world is temporarily good-
    evil.
Help us, Ultimate God, to observe and write effectively
    in a good-evil world.

LaRue W. Gilleland, editor, *The Journalism Educator*

FOR THE DIVINE PERSPECTIVE

O Lord most high,
Judge of all earth's numberless throngs,
Who sees each tiny millimeter against the sky,
I am diminished by my own sins,
yet enlarged by thy redeeming love.
Give me this day an understanding
of my own true size.
Help me now to seek a clearer sense
of the divine perspective.
Bless me with the confidence to be
neither more nor less than thy servant.
And grant me the strength I need here and now
to measure all things by thy will.

W. C. Fields, director of public relations,
Southern Baptist Convention

FOR CREATIVITY

Almighty God, you have made me in your creative image. Let me bring forth creativity worthy of your name. Teach me to say with you, "Let there be light" — and mean it. Send the Spirit of wisdom to brood over the formless void of my copy — and enlighten it. And when I seek words and images to convey this day's news, let me have in me and before me the eternal Word — him who is the only Good News, Jesus Christ our Lord.

Robert A. MacGill, dean, Cathedral of St. James, South Bend, Ind.

FOR THE POWER OF WORDS

Almighty Father of all men, we thank thee for giving us the power of words that may communicate to our fellow-men the wisdom of thy world, the strength of thy support, and the need for following thy will in building a sane and reasonable environment for those who come after us.

May we as communicators remember our responsibility to ourselves and to each other. May we remember the source of power and our strength. May we ever strive to use our God-given talents in ways that are pleasing to thee, in ways that will add to and not destroy what thou has created.

Give us the courage to seek the truth and to communicate the truth. Soften our biases and our prejudices, and add wisdom to our courage, so that what we speak is beneficial to all mankind.

Mrs. Harvey R. Herbst, president, Theta Sigma Phi

FOR ACCEPTABLE WORK

Dear Lord, may the words of our typewriters and the photos of our cameras as well as the meditations of our hearts be acceptable in thy sight, O Lord, our Strength and our Redeemer.

Carl E. Keightley, editor, *Texas Methodist*

TEN COMMANDMENTS OF JOURNALISM

1. SERVICE. The good newspaper does its best to tell each person in its community every day what the person desires to know, provided the information is legitimately public information.

2. INDEPENDENCE. The good newspaper permits no obstacle to deflect it from what it conceives to be its duty. Editorially it voices its honest convictions, nothing more and nothing less. It takes orders from no person and no interest save the public interest.

3. COURAGE. The good newspaper will not adopt a weak, time-serving attitude on any question. It will express its convictions with unmistakable clearness.

4. HONESTY. The good newspaper will tell the truth under all circumstances and will not lend or sell its columns to others for the dissemination of untruths. No advertiser is permitted to make any sort of misrepresentation to its readers, and it provides itself with ample safeguards to make this rule effective.

5. ACCURACY. The good newspaper, realizing that it must be reliable or forfeit its claim to public confidence, studies the reliability of each of its many sources of news or other material that appears in its columns. It detects and weeds out blunderers and prevaricators as quickly as possible from among those who serve it.

6. ENTERPRISE. The good newspaper strives continually to be a better newspaper. Never wholly satisfied with what it has accomplished, it is always engaging in new undertakings.

7. SOUND JUDGMENT. The good newspaper tries unceasingly to be right. Its views are sane, and it endeavors to make its knowledge as broad, as complete, and as nearly accurate as humanly possible.

8. HUMAN INTEREST. The newspaper that deals too much with abstractions and too little with everyday incidents that give life its flavor may be awfully good in the sense that it is awfully proper, but it is not a good newspaper.

9. LIBERALITY. The good newspaper has no prejudice, but it has an ample store of convictions. It finds looking for something to commend more fun than looking for something to condemn.

10. OPEN MINDEDNESS. The good newspaper continually grows in knowledge and wisdom, just as does a good man. Every opinion held by either is subject to revision on short notice.

Charles H. Dennis, editor emeritus,
Chicago Daily News

FOR THE WRITERS OF WORDS

God, you called some to be teachers, and some to be preachers, and some to be deacons, and drawers of water, and hewers of wood; and some who were fit for none of these worthy occupations you called to be writers of words. We ask your grace upon such as these.

Help them, God, to get their stories factual and straight. Guide their fumbling fingers on the typewriter keys, and for whatever good it may do, strengthen the connection between their fingers and their minds. And such hearts as they have, bid them use them freely that their printer's ink might evoke the flowing not of blood but of fellowship.

Give them a good story now and then, to keep their editors civil, their readers happy, and their minds off their own degradation. And when that day comes for their final thirty-dashes, mercifully grant them just a glimpse of your glory before they travel to that eternity to which they have been consigned so frequently by so many.

Vic Jameson, *Monday Morning*

A MAGAZINE EDITOR'S PRAYER

Great Father with the compassionate heart,
help me to do my task today with patience,
with kind understanding,
and, if it is possible,
with at least a small degree of wisdom.

Grant that I may be wise enough to evaluate these
    offerings
with something more than mechanical procedure,
that I may be penetrating enough
to look beneath the surface of words
into the heart of meaning
and that I may weigh and evaluate
with a perception that is both wise and kind.

Grant that I may approach each manuscript
with expectancy and high hope,
and that even in the routine of the day
I may still maintain the spirit of the discoverer.

Walter G. MacPeek, author, New Brunswick, N.J.

MERCY FOR AN EDITOR

O Lord of the pen and the press,
of this old typewriter
and that remorseless deadline,
make me an instrument of good news.
Make me brave to speak truth as I see it
but — oh, Lord! — hold down my editorial ego.
Give me joy in helping others speak truth
as they see it,
and honesty in groping
for the truth beyond us all.
Don't let me get too dull — Lord, no!
but deliver me from an addiction to sensations.
Help me to sift through all reported happenings
and to separate the redeeming from the trivial.
Help me to be patient with my colleagues
who must be heroic
to put up with my own shortcomings.
Help me to cope with all these machines
and to hold high the human purposes above them.
Don't let me swear too often at the postal service
and all the other inefficient works of government
(which remind me of the inefficiencies
of certain journals and certain churches I know!)

Turn me on to the talents
of the new writers and artists:
let me help to swell the stream of creativity.
Let me give voice
to the unrepresented and the oppressed:
enlist me in the struggle for justice and peace.
When my imagination sags
and my information staggers,
help me to be a humble beggar among fellow editors
and all sorts of people who can lift me up
and straighten me out.
Lord, be merciful to me, an editor.

Alan Geyer, editor, *Christian Century*

A WRITER'S PRAYER

It's about this typewriter of mine, Father.
When I strike a certain key,
I notice that the bar comes up and strikes the ribbon,
and the identical letter I selected
appears on the copy paper.
Why can't I be like that?
What I'm asking for is power and wisdom
to carry out your will in my life.
I know that except you inhabit the journalist,
he labors in vain that writes.
Except you work over the story,
the typewriter clacketh but in vain.
Help me to write what you wish me to write,
and to leave it at that:
no more, no less;
through Jesus Christ,
the author and finisher of our salvation.

Sherwood Wirt, editor, *Decision*

PRAYER OF A PRISON
NEWSPAPER EDITOR

O Father, let the readers of my articles see through any pomposity or verboseness the articles may possess and receive a germ of goodness from them. And let my interpretation of a situation never be one-sided, but show both sides, for I am only your tool to enlighten my fellow man of earthly things.

If I should weaken in these endeavors, Lord, remember that your servant is only human, and instill in him the belief that faith and hard work can accomplish all things.

And, Father, if there are those over me, who would limit me in these endeavors, put in their hearts the knowledge that you are over us all.

Floyd King, editor, *The Menard Time*

A BLACK REPORTER MEDITATES

When the press conference bores you
and the speaker ignores you;

when Toms accuse you and militants abuse you,
when the publisher hates you and your editor berates
   you,

when the coffee is stale and your copy is pale,
when the protests get bigger
and they call you "nigger,"

when your byline is buried
and Whitey's is carried;

when critics get louder while the brothers grow
   prouder
when journalistic objectivity colors what you really see
and the pay ain't what it ought to be:

then it's time, you ought to figure
to come alive with new freshness and vigor,
ignore the cries of "Tom" and "nigger";
forget about deadlines and be a digger.

It's been a bad day, God, I'm sorry to say,
listen, please as I pray:
Lord, I have a dream
that's out of sight —
I'm checking out
you take over tonight!

Millicent Brown Fauntleroy, reporter, *Davenport Times*

A COLUMNIST'S PRAYER

Lord of Truth, grant that I may always speak the truth.

Don't let my own notions get confused with the way it actually is.

Don't let me convey the impression that there are any easy answers to life.

Help me to be understandable, but keep me from oversimplification.

Season my words with love, compassion, and understanding.

And yet, when truth brings criticism down upon my head, help me not to compromise it, and adulterate it — just for the dubious reward of being uncontroversial.

Give me sound opinion on current problems, but may I always differentiate between what I think and what actually may be right. Let phrases like: "As I see it," and "It is my considered opinion," season my comments.

May I so live that those who believe in me may never be disillusioned. If sometimes I lack clarity, at least give me sincerity. But, if it be thy will, give me both.

And may I write, not to impress, but to inform, inspire, and occasionally, to entertain.

May I use the Golden Rule, which might read: "Write unto others, as you would have others write unto you."

And season my life and my work with a love like unto thine own. Give me frankness without cocksureness; help me to be picturesque without being flowery, and honest without being a prude.

In the name of him who was and is the Truth.

Billy Graham, columnist, *Chicago Tribune-New York News* Syndicate

A TRAVEL WRITER'S PRAYER

Our Father in heaven, as believers in the Lord Jesus Christ, his resurrection and his return, we know our only purpose here is to serve thee.

Therefore, God, work through us as journalists that thy ways may be fufilled.

We pray for mighty and mysterious things to occur; that thy name be lifted up; thy kingdom advanced — And in the blood shed by Christ, that the devil be continuously defeated.

Let thy guidance be present, thy forgiveness of sins continuous.

Roger Swanson, travel news editor, *Kansas City Star*

FOR COURAGE

Endow us with courage, we beseech thee, O Lord; courage that is born out of loyalty to all that is noble and worthy; that scorns to compromise with vice, ignorance, or injustice in any walk of life — and which knows no peace when right and truth are in jeopardy; that the words of our mouths, the meditations of our hearts and the actions of our lives may be acceptable in thy sight; O thou our strength, our redeemer, and our one and eternal hope.

Lester Kinsolving, religion columnist,
National Newspaper Syndicate

A PRISON EDITOR'S PRAYER

Almighty God, who art the refuge and the fortress of all who live in limbo, strip me of bitterness and self-pity. Sustain me in my loneliness and safeguard me from despair. Let me recognize that adversity is the sternest test of all and give me strength to overcome it in spirit and deed.

Give me the wisdom and the skill to convince my readers of these truths and the saving grace of humor to brighten and sustain them. Help me bring courage and hope to those who have broken thy commandments.

Give me the ability to reach beyond these walls to the outside world. Let me remind them that convicts are human beings. Help me make America aware of the penal reforms that are needed and convince them that the reforms are according to your divine plan.

Give me pride in craftsmanship. Help me accept criticism without rancor, and stand steadfast against proposals and orders I know in my heart to be wrong.

I thank you, Lord, for the privilege of serving thee in my own humble way, and I pray that I may be worthy.

Charles Clayton, journalism professor,
Southern Illinois University

A CAMPUS NEWSPAPER
ADVISER'S PRAYER

To whatever Spirit watches over advisers:

Allow me to see the truth of issues in a world of many sides and conflicts. In an age of much fermentation and fragmentation of values, help me to see what must be a right course of action.

Give me strength to stand firm in that knowledge of a right course and in that action against powerful forces, against my own emotions, against my own human weakness.

Help me to convey to all sides what is true, what is fair, what is just, and what, therefore, must be printed.

Enable me to show that truth emerges from fact, reason and logic, not from emotion or demagoguery, and it must be sought actively and responsibly.

Finally, give me the ability to teach students and others that the wide dissemination of that truth, once found, is greater than any personal interests because it is the rationale on which human society must base its hopes for survival.

John H. Knowles, chairman, journalism department, Kansas State College

A PRAYER FOR NEWSMEN

O Thou who art
the Truth and the Publisher of news
far greater than we puny mortals can
either comprehend or narrate
except in part, deliver us from the smug sophistication
   of this our day
where it is cute to be cynical
where it is profitable to be compromising,
strategically safe to be timid,
convenient to be clever,
where it is considered more virtuous
to take potshots at pygmies
than to do battle with entrenched giants.
At least,
save this moment
from being a hollow gesture to custom or convention.

Incite in us
a reverent awe of Thee that is the beginning of wisdom
Illumine us
with insight to understand
that the evil of our world,
which we pretend and profess to abhor,
is nothing less than the accumulation
of all devices that are unrighteous with us as
   individuals,

Be constant to remind us, however, that
goodness is just as real as malevolence,
and integrity just as prevalent as expediency.
Help us to be
faithful stewards of a noble estate,
courageous citizens of a free land,
who take stubborn moral pride
in telling the news.

James P. Clements, religion editor, *Houston Chronicle*

FOR A NEW BEGINNING

O God, inconceivable to our minds but ever-present in our hearts, we turn to you, trusting not in our goodness but in your mercy to assure us of a hearing. Forgive us, Lord, for all the things we did last year which we ought not to have done; And also for the things we should have done, but did not get around to doing. For impatience, irascibility, intolerance, and anger; for many subtle forms of dishonesty and deceit; for being very attentive to our own wants but unmindful of the needs of others; for being too busy to take time to be kind: forgive us, Lord.

Help us to face the year ahead with hope, with courage, and with a renewed determination to do the right thing.

It is not easy for us to do this, for we are weary, Lord. Weary of confrontation and clashes between generations, division and distrust between races. Weary of inflation, taxes, traffic jams, shoddy workmanship, polluted air, pornographic movies and puerile TV shows. Weary of caring. Refresh our spirits, Lord. Renew our capacity for compassion. Restore our commitment to justice. And please God, let there be peace.

Grant to newspapermen, and all who work in the communications media, a lively awareness of their fallibility and a keen sense of their obligation to be fair and truthful. We do not have the nerve, Lord, to ask your blessing on the poor, the oppressed, the aged, the sick, the lonely, the handicapped and the hurt, for we know that they already are the special objects of your fatherly concern. What we do ask is that we who are well and strong and solvent may remember that it is up to us to act in the world as your servants and stewards, giving practical expression to your loving purpose toward the least of these our brothers.

We thank you for your great patience with us in the past. Bear with us, Lord, and we will try to do a little better.

Louis Cassels, religion writer, United Press International

A SUBURBAN EDITOR'S PRAYER

O Lord, help me to face each new day with the dedication that serving my community is the most important undertaking that faces me. Help me not to be discouraged with the problems that come across my desk or reach me via the telephone, but give me the patience to listen to both sides of each story. Then endow me with the knowlegde and understanding to present the facts to my readers.

Give me the time to listen to my readers no matter how trivial their queries or suggestions might be, and help me in some way to assure them that their problems are also my problems and that finding a solution is just as important to me as it is to them.

Help me to have steadfast faith in the community leaders and public officials who have been selected or have volunteered their services to make our community a better place in which to live, but also give me the courage to let them know when they are not fulfilling their responsibilities.

Make me a booster of my community and one who will recognize the good things that are being done by so many, as well as the bad things that are being perpetrated by a few.

And, above all, help me not to quit when the going gets tough, but give me the strength to meet each challenge as it arrives. May the contributions of my time and that of my staff work for the good of the community and all of our residents.

Paul D. Coffman, editor, *Star-Sentinel,* Melrose Park, Ill.

A NEWSPAPERMAN'S CREDO

I believe in the integrity of the newspaperman to the facts and events with which he is dealing. He must give the event as it actually happened, the facts as they actually are, to the best of his descriptive power. His obligation to what actually happened is as exacting as the obligation of a historian, and his regard for evidence must be as scrupulous.

He has also the obligation, whenever the facts or events do not speak for themselves, to give the frame within which their meaning becomes clear. This may be a frame of history, or a broader interpretative frame of fact. In doing this he must make clear the distinction between fact and event on the one hand and his own opinion on the other.

In deciding what to include or omit he must use to the best of his ability the test of what is newsworthy in the minds of his readers, and what is of importance in the flow of events. He must resist the temptation of including or excluding on the basis of what will help or harm whatever team he is on and whatever crowd he runs with.

This means that he must give a hearing even to unpopular causes, including those which he may himself detest. He has the obligation to keep the channels of the press open for a competition of ideas, since only through such a competition will the people be able to arrive at their own decisions of what is right and good.

In any contest of opinion he has the obligation to state, as fairly as he knows how, the opposing viewpoints. At the same time, if he is presenting opinion in an editorial or a column, he has the obligation to set forth his own position honestly and forthrightly as his own, regardless of the consequences.

Beset as he inevitably will be by favor-seekers, special interests, press agents, public relations men, and operators of all kinds, he must keep himself scrupulously independent of their favors and pressures. This means that he must be strong enough to make himself unpopular with those who can smooth his path or make life pleasant for him.

He must resist all pressures from outside, whether they be from advertisers, government officials, businessmen, labor organizations, churches, ethnic groups, or any other source which has an effect on the circulation or revenue of his paper. This applies whether the newspaperman is a publisher, editor, reporter, reviewer, or columnist. Since the danger in many cases is that he will anticipate the pressures before they are exerted, and censor a news story, review, or opinion which may hurt circulation or revenue, he has the obligation to resist the voice from within himself which tells him to play it safe.

His responsibility is to his craft and to the integrity of his mind.

Max Lerner, columnist, *New York Post*

FOR INCREASED SENSITIVITY

Dear God,
thank you for placing me in a position
where I can serve you;
direct me so that I may do a good job.
Let me sort the important from the unimportant
and divide my time wisely.
Let me have patience and understanding
in dealing with people.
Help me to apply equal and fair standards
in judging news.
Help me to be positive and constructive
in my approach to a story,
and sensitive to the needs and wishes of my readers.

Don't let my job become routine.
Help me always to re-evaluate
and aim for improvement in my work.
Let me constantly search for things
which have meaning.
Let the extra work be compensated by a job well done.
Don't let me be burdened
by too many demands upon me.
Let me separate my business self,
where I am wanted because of my position,
from my personal self,
where I am wanted because I am me.
Let my efforts bring you the glory.

Helen T. Gott, religion editor, *Kansas City Star*

COMBAT CORRESPONDENT'S PRAYER

Arm me, O God,
with courage to go where the story goes,
yet fear of becoming calloused to the horrors of war;
detachment that never loses sight of basic issues,
yet involvement that shares
the thoughts and fears of individuals;
purpose in the knowledge that free men must know,
yet a sense of divine purpose
that always recognizes war
as the failure of men to know thee.

Steve Bell, war correspondent,
American Broadcasting Company

FOR GUIDANCE

Heavenly Father, we ask thy blessing on our work. Guide us in our thought, lead us to find thy will, forgive us when we fail thee. In weariness we ask thy strength; in seeking we ask thy hand; in thought we ask thy mercy. Before ourselves we ask thy blessing, on those who depend on us, our children, our people, our land. Make us to be worthy of them. Thou knowest our inward stress, Eternal Father. Give us, we pray, thy peace.

Eugene Patterson, managing editor, *Washington Post*

GO WITH US IN OUR WORK

Father of us all, for all the splendors of this busy world, we thank thee.

For the freedom we enjoy, for every dream that comes to birth, for the friendships we cherish, for the opportunities to serve our fellows, for all thy guidance all the way, we praise thy holy name.

Thou hast called us to a significant task in this world of thine, the task of reporting facts about thy daily working among men, of speaking boldly from the heart of things we believe to be true and honorable, of leading the nation to higher levels of living.

Go with us in our work. Give us the faith in thee and in humanity which can help keep a people free. Inspire us and lead us so that we may carry with us added wisdom and a renewed determination to be obedient unto the heavenly vision.

Be thou, we humbly pray, our guide and portion forever.

Dwight Marvin, editor, *Troy* (N.Y.) *Record*

A PRAYER TO RECOGNIZE GOD

Almighty God, we recognize that of ourselves we are impotent to achieve the radiant goals which thou hast inspired us to set for ourselves. Let us not say of our best deeds that we accomplished these with our own puny powers. Thy hand, unseen and often unrecognized, has been upon our shoulders in good works, and we bow to thee.

For our freedoms and our strength in freedom, we thank thee because thou hast been more vigilant of our liberties than we ourselves. Awaken us. Open our eyes to the swinging blade of arbitrary power and ignorance and bless the steel with which we go to battle.

In the name of him who wrote but one story, and that with his finger on the ground in Galilee, let us not believe of ourselves that we are divinely appointed to be throwers of stones because we are sinless. First among our sins is that of self-righteousness. Open our eyes that we may see ourselves, not necessarily as others see us, certainly not as we see ourselves, but verily, in thy truth, as we are.

102

We do not ask to go unfettered. We willingly wear bonds of thy making. Make us prisoners of a lively conscience. Make us captives also of an acute sense of justice toward our fellow man. Bind us to the post of journalistic duty.

Carl Lindstrom, editor, *Hartford Times*

A PRAYER FOR PEACE

Heavenly Father, as newspaper editors, we hope that we may assist in finding a solution to the unrest that has troubled our nation and the world. Give us guidance in striving to put to rest the difficulties that have disturbed our country and to assist us in bringing about understanding in our divided communities. May we also look forward to that day when peace will be within the grasp of all men and when people of all persuasions may pursue a common goal of happiness and love. Give us, Heavenly Father, the courage to seek these attainments for all thy children.

Arthur C. Deck, editor, *Salt Lake City Tribune*

A NEWSPAPER EDITOR'S PRAYER

Father of all, thou who art the source of all truth and knowledge, we pause before thee to acknowledge the responsibility of our mission and to offer gratitude for the teachings that make it possible for us to perform with integrity and honor.

Instill in us a love of honest work and hatred for falsehood. Give us the tools to help preserve the wisdom and sanity of this world and the honest courage to refuse to compromise thy higher law of truth for the hope of immediate gain.

Grant unto us thy guidance and keep our hands to the tasks of imparting knowledge and truth that all men may be free.

Felix McKnight, editor, *Dallas Times Herald*

A BROADCASTER'S CHRISTMAS PRAYER

Our Father in Heaven, we bow humbly before thee to express our gratitude for our many blessings and to pray for thy continued guidance. We are mindful of the weighty responsibilities that are ours by virtue of our opportunities for serving thy children. We acknowledge thy hand in the gifts of these great instruments for sharing sights and sounds the world over. We thank thee for the men and women whose skills and dedication have perfected our mechanisms and given us unmatched tools with which to meet the needs and wants of mankind in the realms of the intellect and spirit.

Grant, our Father, that in exercising our stewardship over these great forces, we may have wisdom and discernment in responding not alone to the wants of the people, but in a larger sense, that we may be inspired by thee to recognize the needs of humanity and to devote our finest talents in offerings that will be worthy of a place upon the altar of lasting service to our fellow men.

Father, we would share in the great mission of securing "peace on earth and good will toward men." Help us to preserve the vision of our potential which bursts upon us like a great light as we reach the ascending summits of our best performance. Be thou our guide so that we will not lose our way in the Valleys of Mediocrity.

Our Father, attune our ears to the sounds of the heavenly hosts, and sharpen our focus so that we too may see the new star on the horizon, everlastingly shining for all who believe, for it is the star of faith. We ask this prayer humbly, in the name of thy son, Jesus Christ.

Ralph W. Hardy, vice-president,
Columbia Broadcasting System

A PRAYER OF GRATITUDE

Our Father, creator of all mankind, we thank you for our lives, for the array of the heavens, the order of the planets and for our own earth, world, continent and nation.

We are grateful, in a very special way, for the life of your son who lived and died for freedom, justice, love and salvation of all who are created in the image of his Father.

We come before thee with humility and with our trifling gifts. Your gifts to us have been immeasurable. To some of us you have given the gift of journalism. We are indeed indebted to your dispensation of grace.

You have, in your benign graciousness, told us to overcome arrogance, bias, greed, hate and racism. The commandments have been for us to seek out the truth, despise evil, and ferret out the good news that Jesus Christ is the resurrection and the life.

W. A. Reed, religion news editor, *Nashville Tennessean*

A PRAYER FOR ENDURANCE

Give us courage to stand for the right when it is unpopular and openly scorned. Show us, above all, how to earn our own honorable living and provide for all the varied needs of life, without sacrificing character and personal integrity. Sustain us while we are trying to work out the details and the application of these general principles for ourselves, and grant that our life in business and profession, as well as our life in church, may lead us to the feet of our Master.

Richard K. Morton, *The Student Prayerbook*

THE BROADCAST NEWSMAN'S CREED

My job is news, reporting it and interpreting it. To this assignment today, I pray that I may bring honesty, integrity, and a respect for the public that I serve. The truth to me shall be precious, and thus treated; and because it is precious, I will share it with others, for truth is the wealth of freedom.

I will strive to set aside prejudice during the hours that I give to this hopeful task, for prejudice is a whip that scars the mind.

My loyalty shall be to the fact, and my purpose to make it known.

But to that rigid loyalty, I pray that I may bring a compassionate understanding of the importance of the fact to the peaceful and faithful pursuits of the people who dwell in this place.

Whatever talent I have, I will give to relating faithfully this day's events. And this evening, when it is done, I will seek tomorrow and hope to find in it the reward of yesterday.

National Association of Broadcasters

A PRAYER FOR DIRECTION

God and Father of all, who from the beginning came to bring light and truth and love to man, by the Word, grant to us who deal with words and images, such a reverence for them, that through careful and honest work, we may keep the coinage of our language sound. Give us humility to realize that we are called, not to be perfect but to be clear, not to be infallible but to be fair. Direct those who in this our generation speak where many listen, who write what many read, and who show what many see, that they may do their part in making the heart of our people wise, its mind sound, and its will righteous.

David B. Collins, dean, Cathedral of St. Philip, Atlanta, Ga.

FOR A SENSE OF VOCATION

We thank thee, O God, for thy gifts of poets and writers, for those who have scorned delights and lived laborious days, in poverty and isolation, at the call of letters. We praise thee for all excellence of impression and all communication of insight, for all challenge to frivolity and all deepening of wisdom through writing and reading. Grant to writers and journalists in this generation a sense of their vocation, skilled craftsmanship in words, careful scholarship, and sound judgment. May they rejoice in a new understanding of thy creation and redemption in all they read and write, guided in its use that it may be to thy glory. So may the beauty of words be seen as the beauty of holiness, through him who came among us as the living Word. Amen.

Based on Sarum Primer

5825H